HOW WE SHOULD
RULE OURSELVES

HOW WE SHOULD RULE OURSELVES

Alasdair Gray

ALASDAIR GRAY
AND
ADAM TOMKINS

CANONGATE
Edinburgh · New York · Melbourne

First published in Great Britain in 2005 by
Canongate Books Ltd, 14 High Street,
Edinburgh EH1 1TE

1

British Library Cataloguing-in-Publication Data
A catalogue record for this book is available on
request from the British Library

ISBN 1 84195 722 4

Typeset by Palimpsest Book Production Ltd, Polmont, Stirlingshire
Printed and bound in Great Britain by Clays Ltd, St Ives plc

www.canongate.net

Contents

Preface

The authors of this pamphlet first met on Calton Hill,
Edinburgh, on 9 October 2004 when attending a
demonstration called by the Scottish Socialist Party. We
were there to boycott and protest at the official opening by Queen Elizabeth of a new Scottish parliament
building. The royal ceremony, we felt, was deliberately
designed to remind the Scots and their elected representatives in parliament that even after devolution
Scotland continues to be ultimately governed through
distant offices of the British Crown. But if we take a
wider view most of England, Wales and Northern
Ireland are ultimately governed through distant offices
of the British Crown.

Our prime minister and his cabinet, the civil service,
police, secret services, armed forces and courts of law
– that is, all principal branches of the British state –
owe their allegiance to, and derive their powers from,
the British Crown. It is why some politicians think folk
admitted to British citizenship will be more likely to
obey British laws if they swear allegiance to the Crown;
though native Britons needn't.

Most people living on these islands believe that the
Crown and its powers are effectively controlled by
elected parliaments and that as a result Britain may be
called a democracy. This pamphlet aims to undo these
illusions. We believe the best kind of government is
open, genuine parliamentary democracy. Here we set
out the principles upon which our political beliefs are
founded, say something of the history of these islands

to explain how we arrived at our present state, and set out an agenda for republican constitutional reform.

This publication is one of many recent political tracts aimed at British voters, among them Harris's *So Now Who Do We Vote For?* and Candappa's *The Curious Incident of the WMD in Iraq*. With this year's General Election in mind, the authors had neither time nor space to speak of the European Federation or global corporations. We believe that a world of equally independent republics, none with larger populations than England or California may be the only possible corrective to a world ruined by huge profit-making companies. That may become the argument of a longer book for which this is a rough sketch.

A personal note about the authors: both are men of the left but neither belongs to, nor endorses, any political party. *How We Should Rule Ourselves* is not an argument for socialism: it argues for a republic. It argues for political freedom, democracy and responsible government. A number of our arguments develop ideas first presented in Adam Tomkins' book, *Our Republican Constitution* (Hart, 2005). Both authors thank Rodge Glass for his help with this pamphlet.

CHAPTER 1

A Republican Vision

We want all people to rule themselves through democratic institutions, and explain in the following pages why these should also be republican. The voters within the United Kingdom may eventually decide whether their nations stay combined under one federal parliament, as in the USA and Germany, or elect independent parliaments that collaborate without a single governing body, as happens in the Nordic Union composed of Denmark, Norway, Sweden, Finland and Iceland.

Republicanism has a long, illustrious history. It can be traced back to Ancient Greece and the ideas of Aristotle. Greek practices were revised for Rome by a quartet of great authors – Cicero, Livy, Tacitus and Sallust – who remain leading authorities in republican thinking. Their ideas were taken into the modern age by Machiavelli, whose *Discourses on Livy* exerted enormous influence in the revolutionary climate of seventeenth-century England. An explosion of republican writing happened between the early 1640s and late 1680s, when civil war in England, Scotland and Ireland involved radical democrats, Cromwell's New Model Army and the Levellers. This was the time of James Harrington, John Milton, Algernon Sidney and John Locke. The writings and deeds of these extraordinary men (not all of whom were republicans) hugely influenced the founders of the American republic. Madison and Jefferson brilliantly combined the thinking of Harrington and Sidney with the work of Montesquieu to justify the first and greatest republican revolution, in

1776. It tore most of North America away from the British Crown and made the United States an independent nation.

Four great principles have emerged from this rich heritage. They are the principles on which our argument for British republics rest. They are:

1. Popular Sovereignty instead of Monarchy
2. Political Freedom – the right not to be dominated
3. Social Equality – freedom of choice
4. Governments Accountable to the Public

Let us say something more about these before we proceed.

Popular Sovereignty instead of Monarchy

Power has to come from somewhere. For monarchists it comes from the top – from a king or queen. In an absolute monarchy like Tsarist Russia it stays there. In what is known as a limited or constitutional monarchy it is allowed to filter down, first through courtiers, then through ministers. This is what happened in Britain. Power started with the Crown and over the centuries it has trickled down, first through an aristocratic House of Lords, later joined by a mercantile House of Commons, and now through the leaders of our mass political parties.

For republicans, by contrast, power comes from the bottom. It comes from the people who, as citizens, delegate it upwards to the institutions of government. The US Constitution rests on this basis. Its first words are 'We the people'. Under their constitution, the American people delegate power to the states, which in turn delegate power to the federal government of the United States. Such delegated power is limited. Government may do *only* those things which the people have expressly permitted it to do. This is, at least, the theory on which the US was based – whether that theory is realized in today's America is a different issue. In the republican ideal, the people are sovereign and the government is limited. This is the opposite of what happens in a monarchy.

We believe that sovereignty belongs to the citizens of a nation. There should be no political or legal authority superior to the people. Government is for the benefit of the people, not the other way around. We the people lend power to a government in order to help ourselves – power is not the government's to keep.

Political Freedom – the right not to be dominated

To possess political liberty is to be free from domination; to be free from being ruled by those who get more power to do as they wish by restraining others. The restraints of a fair and open legal system do not deprive us of freedom but bestow it. It does so by preventing us 'being subject to the potentially capricious will . . . of another'. The worst kind of unfreedom, of course, is slavery, where people are the legal property of those who capture or buy or inherit them. Owners of slaves could use them as they wished, and all who helped them escape were guilty of theft. Some writers used to say that slaves with good masters had as much freedom as they needed. But for republicans, the dominion of even the kindest and most benevolent man is bad if he can interfere with his underlings without asking leave, without scrutiny, without risk of penalties.

A modern example of dominion is Queen Elizabeth II. British law gives her the right to appoint whomever she wishes as prime minister. She may legally dismiss the government at any time for any reason or for none. She can refuse assent to any bill passed by the Houses of Parliament. She may do these things without asking leave, without scrutiny, without risk of penalty. For over two centuries unwritten customs have restrained British monarchs from using these powers except in extraordinary circumstances, while other unwritten customs result in royal powers being transferred and used by prime ministers, sometimes also without public scrutiny or risk of penalty. We will describe in later chapters how this state came about and how it is being abused to increase the dominion of the Crown's government.

Social Equality – *freedom of choice*

Poverty is one of the forms of insecurity most likely to render a person liable to domination. In today's world, freedom is as seriously challenged by the increasing differences between the richest and poorest people employed by private companies as it is by states and governments. Our world is scarred by staggering differences in material conditions, which, as the French political philosopher Jean-Fabien Spitz has put it, 'cannot be proven to function for mutual advantages, so that liberty's main enemy is not only the state but also the extraordinary concentrations of private wealth and power which constrain those who are not members of the wealthy inner circle'. Republicans since at least the time of Harrington have been concerned with the threat to freedom that is posed by such material inequality. Harrington and his seventeenth-century ally Henry Neville devoted great attention to the problem that, as they saw it, 'prosperity and peace could only be achieved when the political system had been adjusted to the distribution of wealth'. Inequality undermines our freedom in two ways: it subjects the poor to the dominion of the wealthy, and those in a state of abject dependence cannot take part in political life in the public-spirited way that a healthy republic requires. A slave's interest is that of his master, not that of promoting the public good. Someone with limited employment opportunities, working overtime at a very low wage, under a contract that lets the boss re-employ him at the end of each month, is hardly likely to complain about abuses he sees in his workplace or bring them to public attention.

Governments Accountable to the Public

Republicans who agree that freedom is non-domination must suggest constitutional changes to existing political constitutions and institutions that would help to secure it. In a large modern state such as Britain, or its parliamentary sub-divisions of England, or Scotland, or Wales, where should we start? Our answer is *with our parliaments*. In 1295, the first common people's parliament was called in England by a king so that he could tax them. Later monarchs used the Commons to quell an unruly Lords, then Lords and Commons combined to chase out one king and replace him with another more amenable. We now need a parliament through which it is possible for ordinary people to *contest* the doings of government. As the philosopher Philip Pettit has urged, we need 'a democracy based not on the alleged consent of the people, but on the *contestability* by the people of everything that government does'. In other words, we want parliaments representing the general public that let the Crown's offices and dominant political parties get away with as little as possible. The first step is to make these offices subordinate to the people by taking off their Crown.

Conclusion

Popular sovereignty, political freedom (as we have defined it), social equality and government fully accountable to the governed are opposed nowadays by monarchy, political domination and government secrecy. We believe that the only way in which the four principles outlined here may be realized in Britain is by abolishing the Crown and instituting republican governments.

CHAPTER 2

Early Democracies and Republics

Whenever many folk have thought democracy a good thing there have been great writers (Plato in Ancient Greece; Hobbes, Burke, Macaulay in England) who argued it was impractical or dangerous or impossible. But parliamentary democracy is the oldest system of government in the world. Despite the Garden of Eden story men and women have never lived in isolated families: throughout the habitable world they have survived in co-operating clusters. On the North Atlantic island of St Kilda twenty or thirty families lived for more than ten centuries in a self-supporting commonwealth, mainly by hunting seabirds and gathering their eggs from ledges on steep cliffs. This dangerous work could only be done in teams. Weekdays began with all the adult men meeting in the narrow main street to decide what should be done and who should do it. This primitive parliament (which can be seen in photographs) lasted until the community, disease-ridden and demoralized through nineteenth-century contact with visiting tourists, dwindled almost to extinction and was evacuated in 1930. Most primitive democracies have now been destroyed by invasion and warfare.

Civilization – a word meaning *city-fication* – did not destroy primitive parliaments everywhere. In rural districts till recent centuries men still met under a tree in their village to arrange local business through discussion. Swiss rural communities, being protected by ranges of gigantic mountains, repelled invaders more easily than most others, so their present democracy evolved from their ancient one with comparatively few disruptions. Elsewhere greed and warfare ensured that struggle for democratic civilizations is the world's most continuing tragedy.

Plato believed the first cities were made when bands of horsemen invaded a land of farmers, enslaved them and built fortified places from which to keep plundering them. Undoubtedly this sometimes happened. William, boss of Normandy, treated England like that. Rome is said to have been founded by an outcast orphan leading a gang of brigands, who acquired women by abducting them from neighbours. But no big town can be supported by simple plundering. It needs a market where produce is collected and distributed – where tradesmen make tools and utensils country folk can't make at home – where a form of policing protects goods from thieves and gangsters. It also needs an agreed system of exchange, by barter, coins or paper money. These many things cannot be achieved or managed by one person, so every town has a council or small parliament, elected by all the citizens, or appointed by a few, or chosen by a local boss. There was always danger of the chief local law enforcer making himself boss. Most very big towns eventually became capitals of kingdoms, but some cities ruled themselves as republics. The earliest to leave detailed records of itself is Athens.

Athenians claimed that theirs was the only Greek state without a ruling class forced on it by foreign invaders. Their first king (they said) had persuaded adjacent tribes to abandon their villages, build a city and live together according to laws they agreed upon while he confined his activities to defending them. From early times the Athenian town council seems to have been all the adult male members meeting on a hillside whose curvature let everyone see everyone else. When the state was rich enough to build a theatre they met in that. From the leading citizens (usually the richest citizens) the council elected a committee (which we would now call the cabinet) to help the king. By the seventh century BCE this committee had dispensed with kings and ruled the state itself. But social change is unending. Growing populations, new sources of wealth, new classes of people ensure that few political constitutions stay unchanged for long. The city became divided into as many political parties as its geographical districts. Tradesmen and small farmers who lived on the higher ground wanted absolute democracy where all could vote equally. On the plain were big landed estates owned by rich lords who wanted a plutocracy ruled by themselves. Along the shore lived fishermen and merchants who wanted a mixed form of government between the first two and stopped either of them getting the upper hand. The city was on the verge of revolution because many common people owed more to the rich than they could repay and could only pay their debts by selling their children into slavery or being enslaved themselves – there was no law to prevent this. When such things had happened in other Greek states a general uprising would give a popular leader dictatorial powers to make things easier for the rebels: which made such tyrants kings in all but name. The Athenian parliament chose Solon: a rich man they all trusted because, though rich, he believed in equal social security for every citizen. He annoyed his followers by refusing the job of tyrant and gave them something better – a new political constitution.

While he was working on it a foreign visitor laughed at him for thinking men's greed and injustice could be restrained by written laws. He said they were like spider webs holding in the weak and poor who got entangled, but torn to pieces by the rich and powerful. Solon answered that men agree when neither side gains by breaking the agreement, and he was making laws for

the Athenians that would be to everyone's advantage to
keep. His laws were not feeble. They neither pandered
to the rich nor satisfied the greed of the majority. He
changed no law or custom that seemed to be working
well and kept as many as he could since complete re-
organisation would cause breakdown of law and order.
He first repealed bad old laws that punished by death
nearly every crime from murder and theft to being un-
employed. He ruled that nobody could be enslaved for
debt and relieved the poor by reducing the interest on
loans. He fixed the value of the currency at a lower
level, so those with heavy mortgages could pay them off.
He left all the offices of state as he found them, in the
hands of the rich, but gave the masses a share in their
own government by ensuring that no war could be fought
or new law passed unless fully discussed in parliament
and approved by the majority. He ruled that all disputes
be settled through trial by a jury containing, like parliament, all adult male citizens, while every citizen had the
right to legally prosecute anyone – even one of the state's
chief officers. Solon said the best cities were those where
most people who had not been wronged were as eager
to punish wrongdoers as their victim.

The Athenian parliament contained no women or
slaves, none of the many foreigners who came to the
city because life there was safer than in their home-
lands, and no citizens who stayed away because they
wanted no say in their government. These last were
called *idiots*, meaning people without ideas. But this state
was so cohesive that when the rest of Greece succumbed
to a vast Persian invasion, the Athenians abandoned
their city to the invaders, took to their ships and fought
back from an offshore island. This tough example led
other Greek states to join them in repelling the Persian
forces. We will not describe how Athens then enlarged
itself into an empire which fell faster than most. But in

later years most European thinkers, even royalist ones, regarded this small democratic republic as the source of their own drama, art, architecture, mathematics, science and philosophy. Many who wanted a better future believed it could only be made under constitutions like the Athenian one.

There were other republics. Ancient Rome was ruled by a senate of landlords called the Equestrians because they could fight on horseback. As in Athens the richest provoked revolts through the high interest they charged on loans to the Proletarians, especially in time of famine. This was inconvenient when Equestrians needed Prole soldiers to help them conquer neighbouring towns, so Proles were mobilized by being permitted to elect two town councillors of their own class, and a senior Equestrian magistrate: in British terms, the Roman senate was a House of Lords with a bit of Commons added. This republic ended after its armies had conquered every land around the Mediterranean and successful generals started fighting each other. The eventual winner became the first Roman emperor who, with army backing, did not need the senate. Later, when invading barbarians cut the Roman Empire into a jigsaw puzzle of new nations, almost all became kingdoms.

Kings were originally warlords – generals ruling defeated people through assemblies of their chief officers. The primitive parliaments of Germany elected a king only when going to war, but warfare became so perpetual in most of Europe that rule by kings and their military followers lasted until the French Revolution (1789–92). The few city-states that survived were plutocratic republics like Venice, whose merchant bankers were the only parliament, and oligarchies like Florence, ruled by bankers with a parliament of trade union leaders. Elsewhere monarchy was so taken for granted that its obvious injustices were thought inescapable.

CHAPTER 3

The Making of Britain

By 1100 German, Scandinavian and French invaders had split what the Romans had called Britain into England, Wales, Scotland and Ireland. Then, as now, England had a bigger population than the other three combined. It also had what was then a modern political constitution: a wholly military one. William the Conqueror, a ruthlessly practical Norman warlord, had made himself king in 1066 and sub-let England's counties to his senior officers, who ruled them as they pleased after promising always to obey him, and that their descendants would always obey *his* descendants. All England was now, by law, Crown property. In Scotland a parliament of local nobles, clergy and town representatives helped monarchs whose only land was private estates, so they were called kings and queens of *Scots*. In south Britain they were called kings and queens of Eng*land* ruling, through a parliament of their biggest military managers called the House of Lords, Saxon natives whose language they despised.

A military government can only exist by continual warfare. The descendants of William and his lords first conquered Wales, ruling it through native princes, so that the Welsh (unlike the English) were allowed to keep their original language. With Welsh help they went on to invade Ireland and some stayed to rule it on England's behalf. They had their own parliament, but their descendants kept becoming Irish, so England's kings felt compelled to reconquer the place for centuries to come. They also battled to take Palestine from the Saracens,

14

and fought a Hundred Years' War to keep hold of
France. They kept failing to conquer Scotland. Few of
William's descendants were as efficient as he and they
frequently fought each other for the Crown, so in four
centuries, all but three heirs to the throne died in battle
or were murdered. But English towns, trades and universities at first flourished without Crown help, and the
lords were not always mere parasites. In 1215 they made
an unpopular king (King John) sign a charter of laws
stating among other things that the Crown would arrest
nobody without charging them with a crime – thus
making monarchs *accountable* to the lords in parliament.
Later kings often broke that law and the lords kept
making them restore it. *Magna Carta* this charter is called,
and its key provisions are still in force today.

Edward I (1297–1307) was almost as efficient as
William. His constant invasions of France and Scotland
needed steadier supplies of money than he could raise
from his House of Lords so at Westminster he established a House of Commons. This represented all
England's inferior local governments – whose members
were chosen by the richest merchants and tradesmen in
county towns, and by small landowners descended from
William the Conqueror's *junior* officers. He also gave
Westminster a legal and civil service to make it easier
to tax them. As the population and prosperity of
England increased this second House, or chamber, found
it could bargain with weak kings by threatening to with-
hold taxation. A time came when laws made by the king
had to be confirmed by both Lords and Commons. The
Habeas Corpus Act, requiring that everyone arrested be
charged with a crime so they could defend themselves
in a trial which must soon follow, had easily been broken
by noblemen within their own jurisdictions. The
Commons made that act the cornerstone of criminal
justice throughout England with trial by jury.

When Henry Tudor came to the throne in 1485 the
House of Lords had been greatly weakened by the Wars
of the Roses, all England's rulers had lost their great
French properties, most English people were sick of
warfare and so was their new king. He liked money
more than anything else and chiefly raised it through
fines instead of taxation. His laws allowed him to fine
lords for having too many followers and to fine merchants and town councils for being unusually rich. This
did nothing for his parliaments but strengthened the
judicial and fiscal Crown offices. He died leaving a huge
fortune to his son Henry VIII, at first a sane and hand-
some man who left the chores of ruling to a deputy,
Cardinal Wolsey. Henry hoped that, through Wolsey's
diplomacy and with papal help, he would become Holy
Roman Emperor of Europe. He also wanted to divorce
his wife, the Spanish king's daughter. When Wolsey
failed Henry got rid of him, took charge of English
politics and emerged as a cruel megalomaniac who so
frightened the two Houses of Parliament that, without
opposition, they passed any law he wanted. (For
instance, they decreed that anyone found guilty of treason to the Crown – meaning anyone Henry thought
guilty – would be boiled alive. After his death both
Houses quickly repealed that law.)

He squandered his father's wealth on elaborate new
palaces, on suits of jewelled clothes and on expensive,
futile wars in France and Scotland. He then got rich
again by cutting off the Church of England from Rome,
taking the Pope's place as its head, disbanding monasteries and selling their lands and buildings to whoever
paid well for them. Though some monasteries contained
clergy as corrupt and greedy as kings and courtiers, they
had still provided poorer people's only healthcare and
education. So Henry's privatization enriched himself
and his parliaments at the expense of the nation's

labourers. It also made some commoners so rich that they were promoted to empty seats in the House of Lords, thus creating a nobility who respected trade as much as fighting. The European discovery of the Americas in 1492 had hugely expanded trade. That England's constitution was now as mercantile as it was military helps to explain why she began acquiring an overseas empire while those of Portugal and Spain declined.

Queen Elizabeth I's courtiers captained their own ships, chose their own crews, and founded settlements in America from which Sir Walter Ralegh brought tobacco and the first potatoes grown in Europe. Sir John Hawkins started what became the world's biggest slave trading company, buying native Africans from greedy chiefs who had conquered them, then selling them in South America, where indigenous people enslaved by Spanish colonists died out so fast that they needed continual replacement. While trading with these colonists English captains enthusiastically captured Spanish ships taking slave-extracted silver home to Europe. Elizabeth apologized to the Spanish king for this piracy, but had shares in it so welcomed the merchant adventurers when they docked in the Thames to the wild cheering of patriotic mobs.

The Union of the Crowns

When Elizabeth died without heir in 1603 Ralegh suggested England become a republic on Venetian lines, with nobility and merchants ruling like directors of a joint stock company. But the Crown was so embedded in England's legal and social system that Lords and Commons invited the king of poor little barbarous Scotland to take the job. Jamie VI of Scotland and I of England was delighted. The Scots in general were

fond of their Stuart kings but had never treated them
with much reverence or obedience. When Henry II had
murmured 'Who will rid me of this troublesome priest?'
some of his knights rode out and slew the Archbishop
of Canterbury. When Jamie had outlawed a troublesome earl (which meant he would reward anyone who
killed the man) the earl burst into the king's bedroom
at Holyrood Palace waving a sword and shouting something like, 'Jamie! Ye cannae do this to me! I won't stand
for it!' Jamie, who dreaded sharp weapons, blubbered,
pulled the sheets over his head and promised not to do
it again. He also hated the Scots Calvinist Kirk whose
ministers thought that, being God's servants, they were
superior to earthly kings. One told him to his face that
he was 'God's silly vassal'. When Jamie got to London
he summoned the minister there and jailed him, saying
that now, with his pen, he ruled Scots whom his ances-
tors could not rule with their swords. Like future Scottish
MPs in the London parliament he was safer as well as
richer in Westminster, where the Archbishop of
Canterbury was his underling. He regarded monarchy
as Richard Nixon regarded the US presidency when he
said, 'If the President does it, it's legal.' But Jamie was
cautious. Though England's parliament never gave him
all the power he wanted, he always gave in before quar-
rels with it reached breaking point.

He carried out a piece of legislation only possible
for a Scots king who also ruled England. Ireland was
again rejecting English rule. The imposition of
Norman, Plantagenet and Elizabethan overlords had
failed to pacify the Irish, who remained as Irish as ever
and were still Catholic! If Catholic Europe ever attacked
England, an Irish army would almost certainly cross the
narrow strait dividing Ulster from the British mainland.
A large invasion of Protestant manual workers might
succeed where English overlords had failed. Few such

workers in England wanted to leave home but Scotland's poverty was continually driving out its surplus population. The French had a proverb: 'Rats, mice and Scots get in everywhere.' So the British Crown confiscated two-thirds of Northern Ireland, the natives were ordered to leave or remain in the condition of servants and their land was given to Protestant settlers, the mass of these being Scots Calvinists. In 1874 the English historian John Richard Green wrote:

> In its material results, the plantation of Ulster was undoubtedly a brilliant success . . . the foundations of the economic prosperity which has raised Ulster high above the rest of Ireland were undoubtedly laid in the confiscation of 1610 . . . The evicted natives withdrew sullenly to the lands which had been left them by the spoiler; but all faith in English justice had been torn from the minds of the Irishry, and the seed had been sown of that fatal harvest of distrust and disaffection which was to be reaped through tyranny and massacre in the age to come . . .

Green cannot have known it would last into the twenty-first century.

Charles I was less cautious than Jamie, his dad. Britain had become an international power. Charles wanted a standing army to assert that power. Previous royal armies had simply been the king's guards and armed servants of the lords, and were disbanded when wars ended. The Commons did not want a standing army because:

1. It would be expensive and they disliked heavy taxes.
2. Britain was adequately protected by a few royal flagships and a private enterprise merchant

   navy whose seamen fought with cannons and
   cutlasses.
3. Charles would almost certainly use a standing
   army in the same way as his brother-in-law, the
   king of France, who abolished parliamentary
   restraint upon the Crown.

Charles therefore did without parliament for eleven
years by not calling it – British parliaments only assem-
ble when the monarch calls. He raised money (though
not enough to pay many soldiers) by selling monopo-
lies and by taxing people directly through Crown offices.
He might still have kept his head had he not tried to
force the English State Church on Calvinist Scotland
by sending in an army. The Scots smashed it. Charles
had to call up a House of Commons to help him pay
for a better army. The Commons did so on conditions
that Charles kept evading which led to warfare throughout Britain, Ireland included. The biggest armies were
English: one fighting for the king, the other fighting for
parliament. Parliament won. In 1649 it beheaded
Charles, disbanded the House of Lords and made
Britain a commonwealth ruled solely by the Commons.
   Eleven years passed before monarchy returned, but
rule by the Commons lasted only four. Its biggest party
wanted to impose Calvinism all over Britain but was
outnumbered by those representing other Protestant
sects. Their bickerings stopped them making important
decisions. Cromwell, general of the most successful army
Britain has known, was made dictator – then called Lord
Protector – and ruled all of England, Wales, Ireland and
Scotland through his chief officers, without making them
titled lords as William the Conqueror had done. So he
now wielded the absolute power Charles I was beheaded
for trying to wield, but wielded it against the will of the
parliament that had chosen him.

Eventually most Britons outside his army came to hate and fear Oliver Cromwell, though few could resist that army. He commanded it so well that in Europe even Catholic kings sought alliances with him. No wonder what remained of the Commons offered him the Crown. He reluctantly refused because the army contained ardent republicans who believed in social equality under God, and some regiments wanted the great English properties broken up so that all who wished might have a farm to cultivate and to feed themselves. Cromwell, himself a landowner, rejected that yet he depended too much on lovers of social equality to start a new monarchy. After his death in 1658 his son Richard (nicknamed Tumbledown Dick) had no will for the job. General Monck, the army's chief remaining major commander, knew that if *he* declared himself Lord Protector most of Britain would gang up against him. He conferred with the remaining Lords and Commons, then invited back the son of the last British king. Charles II was enthroned in 1660 among widespread rejoicing, and the terribly efficient army was disbanded. So England and Wales were once again ruled by three Westminster governing bodies: a House of Lords containing great landowners; a House of Commons representing small squires and town councils; and a Crown that needed both and which both needed.

By the late seventeenth century the Crown was head of:

1. The Treasury, in charge of the mint, from which pensions and bribes were paid and which obtained revenue from customs, excise, post offices and other sources.
2. The Navy and Army, whose upper ranks were

from the richest classes because they bought
their commissions: this made them less efficient
than Cromwell's armed forces, but ensured
obedience to king and parliament.

3. The Secret Fund: used to pay government
   spies. At first noble lords working for the
   Treasury paid them; prime ministers later
   opened a Bank of England account.

4. Public Broadcasting, then done by announce-
   ments from Church of England pulpits.

5. Law Courts with laws which could be changed
   only by King, Lords and Commons agreeing.

This political constitution remains largely in force in
Britain to this day.

Scotland was in the queer position of having its own
parliament and legal system but a king in London, who
overruled the Scots parliament and laws through a few
corrupt lords who taxed inferiors as they liked and fined,
jailed, or executed rivals. Ireland had a parliament
representing only a Protestant minority of lords and
recent settlers.

The restored Stuart king was good for his House of
Lords but nobody much else. Charles II was a lazy
atheist with a big sexual appetite who left governing to
his ministers because it was dangerous for an English
king to meddle with politics. The army and navy
became so inefficient that England's main trade
competitors, the Dutch, sailed into the Thames and
burned ships and royal dockyards. Cromwell's officers,
being unrelated to powerful Scottish families and clan
chiefs, had ruled Scotland with exceptional fairness: the
royal sycophants who now ruled Scotland again tried
forcing the Church of England on their countrymen.
Charles II sent his brother James north to help them,
though James was a Roman Catholic. Staunch

Presbyterians left their kirks, prayed in the open air, and were spied out, shot or hanged by government troops. These were poor, brave, victimized folk, but where their numbers gave them a brief advantage they too treated enemies with intolerant cruelty.

Charles died. His brother James became king of Britain (1685–1701) and tried to make Catholicism legal by proclaiming toleration of *every* religion. Only the Catholic minority was pleased. Episcopalian English and Presbyterian Scots united to expel James and make his daughter Mary's husband, William of Orange, a Dutch Calvinist, the chief executive of Britain and her religion's defender. This made the Church of England supreme south of the Tweed, and a Calvinist Scots Kirk supreme north of it. This resulted in tolerance of most Christians excepting Catholics, who were not allowed to vote or own horses.

A new kind of prosperity allowed the dreamlike unanimity through which lords and clergy, squires and merchants acquired King William. Queen Elizabeth I's richest subjects had jewels, pearls and gold sewn to their clothing because, in a land with no police force, portable wealth was safer on their bodies than in houses and they carried swords to defend it. A century later England had dependable banks, so rich men no longer wore much jewellery or needed to carry swords. In 1694 a Scots businessman called William Paterson persuaded Crown, Lords and Commons to finance war with France by creating their own bank, the Bank of England. This has financed British wars ever since. Great English fortunes were no longer at risk from a monarch or faction who might seize them, if England avoided civil war. But foreign war could increase them, so England has had no civil wars since. The richest landlords and merchants gave their money market the utmost power by putting hereditary millionaires of

Dutch or German origin at the head of Church and
State. So King William, and after him Queen Anne,
and after her King George, signed English acts of parliament which strengthened English trade, English transat-
lantic colonies, English factories in India.

Scotland was excluded from trade with English
colonies; nor could she trade freely with Europe because
until 1678 England was usually at war with Holland or
France. But the financier William Paterson was Scottish.
On a globe of the world he proved that, without English
help, a Scots colony on Panama (where later a canal
was built) could take over all trade between the Atlantic
and Pacific. Most of the Scots Lords and Commons
were so excited by this scheme that they invested heav-
ily in it. Enthusiastic immigrants volunteered to go; ships
for them were built on Clydeside. They went, and found
Panama was uninhabited because the dank air was full
of malarial infection. Adjacent Spanish colonies
attacked them. They asked King William in London for
help. He said he could not give it without disturbing
the peace of Christendom. They beat off the Spaniards
once, begged help from nearby English colonies, who
refused it, and had to surrender. Paterson was one of
the few surviving settlers who got home, leaving behind
about two thousand dead and having lost a quarter of
Scotland's capital. But he had done his best, so the Scots
blamed the English.

The Union of Parliaments

Then Scottish pride took a further knock. Queen Anne
died and the English parliament, without consulting the
Edinburgh parliament, invited her distant cousin
George, the prince of tiny Hanover in Germany, to be
king of all Britain, thus treating Scotland like a
conquered province. The Scots refused to recognize this

new king and almost became an independent nation
again. Alas, only their main religion had democratic
elements. In 1707 the Scots parliament sent commissioners south to negotiate a treaty with England.
William Paterson was a party to the negotiations.

The commissioners returned to Edinburgh with the
following treaty: if the Scots parliament accepted
George Hanover as King of Scots and abolished itself,
England would:

1. Let 45 Scots MPs join 513 English and Welsh
   MPs in the Commons, and 16 Scots lords join
   190 lords in Westminster.
2. Give the Scots parliament an immediate cash
   payment of £398,085 and 10 shillings – the
   exact sum lost by Scottish investors in the
   Panama adventure.
3. Maintain the Scots mint, the Scots kirk, and
   Scots legal system. (The Scots MPs thought the
   Crown would maintain these separate from
   Westminster.)

In case this offer was rejected the English parliament
passed an Aliens Act which would ruin Scottish indus-
try and agriculture by blockading all her trade with
England, Ireland, America, Africa and India. Nor would
she be able to trade with Europe, as England was fighting a victorious war against France, the richest nation
there, without overstraining her credit. If the Scots
insisted on independence England, after defeating
France, could easily invade and rule them through an
army, as Cromwell had done.

Financially the offer was not generous, as England's
treasury would quickly recover its gigantic bribe by
taxing Scotland. The treaty would turn that land from
a nation into a province with only two more Commons

MPs than Cornwall. The Scots clergy denounced it;
Scots towns petitioned against it; in Glasgow, Dumfries
and Edinburgh crowds rioted against it. During the long
debate on it an English spy said the Scots people were
fifty-to-one against. Opposition in the Edinburgh parliament was led by the Duke of Hamilton, who was heav-
ily in debt. Shortly before acceptance was put to the
vote he had secret conferences with the chief nobleman
supporting the treaty, and did not turn up for the election because (he said) he was suffering from toothache.
By a two-to-one majority the Scots parliament voted to
accept the treaty. The same English spy (Daniel Defoe)
then wrote to England's prime minister that:

> The Great men are posting to London for places and
> honours, every man full of his own merit, and afraid
> of everyone near him. I never saw so much trick,
> sham, pride, jealousy and cutting of friend's throats
> as there now is among the Scots noblemen.

Too terrified by a raging mob outside to abolish itself
verbally, the Edinburgh parliament merely *adjourned*
itself, and was reconvened in 1999 as a body almost
totally under Westminster control.

As soon as the Scots representatives joined the
Westminster parliament in 1707 it abolished the Scots
mint and started breaking other terms of the contract.
In England it let local landlords appoint parish clergy:
in Scotland landlords started doing the same, to the
horror of all local kirk elders. Their protests were
ignored. The territory of Highland clans had belonged
to everyone living on them, who were nearly all relations of their chief. Westminster decreed that the chief
now owned the land his clan lived on, so he could evict
his poor relations, with the help of British troops when
that became profitable. Scots lawyers and MPs

complained of these and other violations of a contract freely negotiated between two national parliaments. John Prebble, in his history *The Lion in the North*, gives some of the answers they received:

> Whatever are or may be the rules of Scotland, now she is subject to the sovereignty of England, she must be governed by English laws.

> Have we not bought the Scots, and the right to tax them?

> We have catcht Scotland, and will keep her fast.

But this broken treaty is still the birth certificate of the United Kingdom and Great Britain. On official documents Scotland was now called North Britain, and both North and South got a colourful flag with a bold red English St George's Cross imposed on a thin white Scottish cross of St Andrew – the Union Jack.

Revolution and Reaction

The eighteenth-century parliament was at first dominated by the Whig and Tory parties. Whig MPs mainly represented townsmen and bankers enriched by trade – what Swift called the Financial Interest: they wanted the wars fought with France for mercantile empire in Europe, India, Africa and the Caribbean. Tory MPs represented gentry whose main wealth was in farming, got little by these wars and voted for peace to reduce taxes; but the House of Lords was dominated by great Whig landowners also enriched by trade and banking, so mercantile war was prolonged. A small third party was added to parliament by George III. His grandpa and dad had let parliamentary chiefs govern for them

but George III *wanted* to govern, so used Crown prerog-
atives to create a king's party in the Lords and
Commons. The Scots MPs and Lords joined it because,
having now no power to rule their own nation, they
gladly took bribes to make things awkward for anything
like democracy in England.

When British armies had driven the French from
most of North America, the Westminster government
decided to save on the expense by taxing British colonies
there. Property owners in America were horrified
because they had no representation in Westminster. The
thirteen colonies had each a little parliament, elected
by property owners, with a governor from Westminster
to represent the Crown. If they got rid of the Crown
they could govern themselves, so they did. Four years
before the soon-to-become United States of America
won its war for independence, delegates from each
colony signed a declaration beginning with these words:

> We hold these truths to be self-evident, that all men
> are created equal and endowed by their creator
> inalienable rights; that among these are life, liberty
> and the pursuit of happiness. That to secure these rights
> governments are instituted among men deriving their
> just power from the consent of the governed, that
> whenever any form of government is destructive of
> these ends, it is the right of the people to alter or
> abolish it.

In an earlier draft, the word 'happiness' replaced 'property', because the richest Americans owned slaves who
were property so could not pursue it. Many who signed
this contract assumed 'men' excluded slaves and
redskins, who were not real men so could never be equal.
Others who signed disagreed but saw the declaration
as a true statement of a democratic goal to be worked

for. It introduced a written constitution giving the vote to even small property owners, and ruling that religion should have no part in choosing state officials, and that equality should be maintained by having no hereditary titles, e.g. Knight, Count, Lord. The USA was then a rural republic without big cities, large factories and great fortunes. Senators in some states thought equality and democracy would suffer if the constitution did not limit the amount of money a man could accumulate and pass to his son. The US Congress ruled out that impractical idea.

The Americans had revolted because they had been taxed without parliamentary representation, but many British cities were also not represented in parliament because they had not existed when Edward I first summoned a parliament, while landlords of places where towns and a major city had vanished could put into parliament any MP they chose. Merchants who became rich by trading in African slaves, Caribbean sugar, American tobacco and Indian fabrics bought seats in parliament by bribing town councils. This notorious corruption ('as notorious as the sun at noonday', said members of the king's party defending it), was attacked by both Whigs and Tories when their party was out of office, and staunchly maintained when they got back in. And now an event in Paris made both British parties unite to make *Old Corruption* (as the system was affectionately nicknamed), stronger than ever.

Though still the richest, biggest and most fertile part of western Europe, France was ruled without parliaments by kings and aristocrats who never paid taxes, and now the nation was bankrupt. It had lost so much money by sending troops and ships to help the democratic Yankee revolt that it could not now pay its armed forces, who now also threatened to revolt. To raise money Louis XVI (like Charles I of England)

summoned a parliament in 1788: the first in 175 years.
Its middle-class deputies insisted that the chief lords and
clergy sit and vote in the same chamber as themselves
– that France should have a written constitution like
that of the US – that aristocrats should be taxed like
other citizens – and King Louis be re-titled the *People's
Hereditary Representative*. This Assembly's slogan 'Liberté,
Egalité, Fraternité' (Liberty, Equality, Brotherhood) was
taken by common French peasants and citizens to mean
they too would have a say in how they were ruled.
Whereupon many aristocrats emigrated to Austria and
Prussia, from where they invaded their homeland with
the royal armies of these nations, intending to restore
the old regime. The French Assembly raised a citizen's
army that first halted the invasion, then drove it back.
The People's Hereditary Representative and his wife,
Marie Antoinette, ran off to join the invaders, were
arrested before reaching them, tried for treason, found
guilty and beheaded.

Even at this stage of the French Revolution (as it was
almost immediately called) many British commoners
approved of it, especially those without votes. Edmund
Burke, a British Tory, wrote a pamphlet denouncing it.
He said the old French regime, though vicious in many
ways, was ruled by so many beautiful, polite people that
their vices were forgivable. He pointed out that the
ruling French parliamentary party, through fear of invasion, was now protecting itself by cutting off more and
more of its enemies' heads. He attributed this to the
French using a completely new political constitution
they had written out for themselves – unlike the British
constitution which, since the bloodless 'glorious' revolution a century before, was mainly a matter of gentle-
manly deals in a parliament elected by the few. In 2000
Roger Scruton called Burke's pamphlet 'the first major
statement of modern Conservatism'.

Burke was answered by Tom Paine's *Rights of Man*, which is the first major statement of modern Socialist democracy. He addressed this book to the 95 per cent of Britons denied the vote by their poverty, birthplace or religion. He said the British constitution had not grown naturally, but through many acts of violence, usurpation and injustice legalized by a titled, powerful minority. He said Burke offered them 'perpetual serfdom under the authority of the dead over the living', since Burke was defending the inherited right of this minority to control parliament, enrich themselves, and fight wars for profit. This parliament would never allow reform by people outside it, so people should elect their own representatives to a National Convention that would adopt a written constitution like the USA and France, a constitution declaring:

1. All men are born to free and equal rights, so the only titles should be those of publicly-appointed officials.
2. All political parties must aim to preserve everyone's right to safety, property and liberty, and their right to resist any who endanger these.
3. No single person or group has the right to rule a nation when not entitled by a parliament representing all the people.
4. Members of this parliament should be paid a living wage so that they do not need to take bribes.

In a chapter called 'Ways and Means' he showed how taxes spent on the monarchy, the army and grants to the rich could fund schools, healthcare and old age pensions for all.

As a young politician out of office William Pitt, now Britain's prime minister (1783–1801), had urged those

who wanted parliamentary reform to associate in pres-
sure groups. Many did, but the groups contained more
working-class people than Pitt wanted, especially in
Scotland where manual labourers were more literate.
These Friends of the People (as many groups called
themselves) were enthusiasts for Paine's pamphlet. Pitt
read it in advance and, in order to suppress it, offered
the author 1000 guineas for the copyright. Paine
refused; beat government censorship by having a cheap
edition printed and distributed before it was officially
banned; and avoided arrest for 'sedition' by escaping to
France, where he was made a member of the National
Assembly. Sedition was a crime recently invented by the
British parliament because hitherto the government
could try its critics only on a charge of treason. Under
English law, those found guilty of treason were tortured
to death in a protracted four-century-old ceremony
which English juries detested. The penalty for sedition
was transportation to Australia, which Britain used as
a penal colony – which was as if the US government,
after landing the first men on the moon, had used it as
a jail for suspected terrorists. Paine's book, banned as
seditious, now allowed the arrest and trial of any who
sold or lent a copy. In England many juries found such
people not guilty. Scotland's corrupt judges made sure
everyone accused was transported.

The Modern Era

While the French seized estates from their Crown and
divided them up for sale to the lower classes, Britain's
government did the opposite. In 1790 Britain still had
many 'commons': land that was not private property
where anyone could keep a pig or goat and catch a
rabbit or fish. As a matter of law, the Crown still owned
all England by right of conquest. While it could no

longer seize private property, it started to sell the commons to landlords who fenced them to contain private flocks and crops. Country folk hated these enclosures. Without a nearby common they had to live by labouring for tight-fisted land-owning farmers.

To pay for the war with France Pitt's government raised cash from the poor through taxes on candles, soap, leather, tobacco, windows, while it proposed the first income tax to be paid by the British rich. Income tax was accepted by landlords as they could get their money back by privatizing the commons. Thousands of TRESPASSERS WILL BE PROSECUTED signs went up. Villagers and travellers were prosecuted for poaching on land where, weeks earlier, they had grazed their beasts. Historians call this transformation the Agricultural Revolution. Close behind came the Industrial Revolution. Factory owners complained that they could not supply all the uniforms and weapons the War Office had ordered. The government told them to equip their factories with newly invented machines powered by water or steam. These could be worked by women and children who could be paid much less than men. And if the children were obtained from orphanages and lodged in the factories they could be paid with only scraps and rags.

Pitt prime ministered what was becoming the world's foremost industrial nation, with a spreading railway network, and ships importing material from every continent and exporting machines and goods. Yet the manufacturers, though often rich enough to have friends in parliament, could not vote. Nor could workmen, self-employed weavers, tradesmen or Catholics. Reform was demanded. In 1831 the Commons passed a bill to take seats from places with no voters and give them to towns and cities. The House of Lords rejected the bill. The king dithered. Public protest meetings erupted. Rioters

rioted. A fashionable London tailor with radical ideas
distributed a poster headed GO FOR GOLD! advising
reformers with money in the Bank of England to with-
draw. Many did. This so frightened Britain's money
market that the king and the House of Lords were
forced to make the bill law. Further electoral reform
was to follow in 1867 and again after the First World
War.

In the early 1900s, local governments began to introduce what some called gas and water socialism and
others municipalization. Backed by acts of parliament
they bought out the private companies selling water,
gas, etc, and turned their cities into small republics that
made, owned and managed their own water supplies,
sewage systems, road works, street lighting, transport,
police, schools and public hospitals. In Glasgow the
ruling Liberal party even debated building municipal
housing, at which point ratepayers voted against it, as
it would have deprived them of rents. It was not until
the first Labour government of 1924 that public housing was legislated for.

The Labour party was created by an alliance between
trade unions, a Liberal Scottish nationalist and the
Fabian Society, the last being a group of Marxist civil
servants, town councillors and George Bernard Shaw.
Fabians believed that, without violence or party dicta-
torship, a social revolution could be gradually made by
wise legislation. The Fabians wrote the Labour party
constitution, clause IV of which said an eventual aim
of the Labour party was to have workers owning the
mines and factories that employed them. (The clause
was dropped when Labour became New Labour in the
1990s.) The turbulent years from 1900 to 1940 were
filled by desperate trade unions calling strikes to stop
wages being reduced and by employers fighting back
with lockouts and worse. Industrial production fell.

Trade was halted. Unemployment spread. Private banks
collapsed. One result of this was the victory of the Nazi
party in Germany, which indirectly restored full industrial production to Germany, Britain and France. Their
governments put public money into the arms manufac-
ture and widespread preparations for World War II,
declared in 1939.

Under Churchill, British government *nationalized*. It
took control of every part of the nation's economy –
factories, mines, agriculture and land. Trade unionists
were invited into the cabinet, adequate wages fixed for
all employees, company profits frozen, prices fixed for
the duration of the war. Food and fuel were rationed.
Doctors became the only civilians allowed petrol for
their cars, yet so well was the nation governed that the
generation who grew up during the war were stronger
and healthier than any since public health records
started three generations earlier. Thus was Tom Paine's
and the Fabians' vision of a welfare state managed
under multi-party parliaments realized in 1944 when
the British electorate returned a Labour government
that promised to maintain this welfare state.

And maintain it post-war governments did, for a
while. But since the 1970s the major project of British
government – whether Tory or Labour – has been to
grind down the welfare state, to sideline the trade unions
and to maximize the profits of the few. Under Margaret
Thatcher the state's assets in telecoms, gas, electricity
and water were sold off. John Major sold our railways.
And under Tony Blair all remain in private hands. The
welfare state has been shrunk. The civil service has been
reduced by more than a third since the early 1980s.
Public service has been replaced with private finance
initiatives; public welfare with the mantra of value-for-
money. On New Labour's watch, England has devel-
oped a two-tier health service and tuition fees for

universities. Only in devolved Scotland and Wales have
brakes been applied to the privatization juggernaut.

Yet there is nothing inevitable about the victory of
private capital. As our history shows, Britain once had
common ownership of land, as it had a fine welfare
state and multi-party, open government. Nothing is
forever in politics. Government is shaped – and can be
re-shaped – by its people. If we want to recover the
commons, rediscover the welfare state or restore open
government, *we can*. In the next chapters we explain
how.

CHAPTER 4

Government and Accountability

Good political constitutions confer power and accountability: they give governments the power to act, while making their actions and intentions public knowledge. From our point of view, a good political constitution is one that lets government get away with less. The powerful are less likely to go wrong if their actions and deeds are fully scrutinized and if they openly account for them.

There are several British agencies for making those in power accountable: auditors check public expenditure and ombudsmen hear complaints of maladministration; public inquiries such as those of Hutton and Butler examine scandals like the Iraq war; and there is legal accountability through the law courts and political accountability through parliaments. The British constitution is unusual because it gives precedence to parliamentary accountability. This is true both for Westminster and for the subordinate parliaments of Scotland, Wales and Northern Ireland. This arrangement is based on a simple, unwritten and we think beautiful rule three centuries old. It is that *the government of the day may remain in office for only as long as it continues to enjoy majority support in the House of Commons. The moment such support is withdrawn the government must resign.* This rule secures for Britain its only element of democracy between general elections. In times of crisis it enables our MPs, as a Harvard law professor once put it, 'to throw the scoundrels out'.

The weekly half-hour that Tony Blair must endure at the despatch box in the Commons is a reminder of

this core constitutional rule. He may *seem* the most
powerful man in the country, but the power is not his:
it has been lent to him by those who trust him. Voters
can take it from him in general elections but these
normally occur only once every four or five years, so
to stay in office the prime minister must keep explain-
ing himself to our representatives in parliament. So
must all other government ministers. This is true for
the British government in Westminster as it is also for
the Scottish, Welsh and Northern Irish governments.

Prime ministers and their cabinets usually lead a
political party with a useful majority in the Commons,
so the last government changed by a vote of no confidence was in 1979, when Labour prime minister James
Callaghan was forced to resign. Eleven years later
Margaret Thatcher reluctantly resigned when her cabinet colleagues explained that most Conservative MPs
no longer trusted her. Such rare events are high political drama, but whenever parliament sits all ministers
of state – from the prime minister down – need a majority of MPs to vote for their measures, preferably after
close questioning and debate. Without such majority
support no government can act.

This does not mean that government ministers can
never act without prior questioning and debate. In 1914
the Liberal government declared war first and allowed
parliament to debate the matter second. War was
declared because some years previously the British
government had signed a secret treaty with France,
promising to fight Germany if France was attacked. A
number of Liberals and Tories in the Commons knew
about the treaty, but no one else did. Most people in
Britain were wildly enthusiastic for war with Germany,
then our greatest trade rival. Popular newspapers had
been predicting it with glee for some time, so when
word was announced a happy mob converged on

Buckingham Palace and cheered until the king appeared on his balcony. The only one in the Commons to ask why Britain was at war was Keir Hardie, leader of the then tiny Labour party. It was a question embarrassing for the government because it could not be honestly answered – the fact of Britain's secret treaty with France did not become public knowledge until years afterwards. Luckily for the government, Germany invaded France through Belgium, a nation Britain had an open treaty with, so newspapers and historians could say that Britain fought Germany to help 'plucky little Belgium'.

When, forty years later, Conservative prime minister Anthony Eden instructed British armed forces to invade Egypt in 1956 without declaring war, and hid the fact from both parliament and the public for two days, his feeble justification for it got him dismissed almost at once. When Tony Blair sent British troops into combat in Iraq in 2003 he knew that he had sufficient support in parliament to keep him in power until at least the general election, but parliamentary and popular scrutiny of his part in that war and its consequences has not yet ended.

Stopping government is difficult. Even if parliaments do not always get it right, they remain our best hope. In recent years it has become fashionable to think that the courts of law may be a better alternative. We think this is a mistake.

Assessing the Courts

The role of the courts in Britain has grown so much in the past decade that the judges are beginning to supplant our parliaments as the main authority on what governments may do. Key to this transformation is the Human Rights Act 1998. This act is one of the Blair government's most significant constitutional reforms. It

means that the courts can quash any government decision which they consider to be in breach of human
rights. The result of the act is that government is under
greater judicial scrutiny than ever before. It might be
thought that this would have enhanced both individual
freedom and the legal accountability of government.
The fact is, however, that neither has happened.

In Britain we owe our freedom to parliament, not to
the courts. Parliament has frequently legislated, often in
face of overt judicial hostility, to extend liberty, whether
it be in conferring on women the right to vote, in enact-
ing prohibitions against discrimination, or in providing
for essential welfare services, such as health care and
social security. By contrast, the judicial record in protecting civil liberties in Britain is woeful. The law reports
are littered with cases in which the courts have failed.
To give a few examples:

- The courts upheld the legality of internment
  (detention without trial) in both World Wars.
- In 1935 they held that the police have the power
  to enter and remain on private property even
  when no crime has been committed.
- In 1936 they held that the police have the power
  to obstruct a lawful public meeting where they
  (subjectively) deem it necessary in order to
  prevent a breach of the peace, even where there
  has been no violence.
- In the 1980s they held that Mrs Thatcher had
  not acted unlawfully when she unilaterally
  banned civil servants who worked at GCHQ
  from joining lawful trade unions. Mrs Thatcher
  claimed – wholly spuriously – that she was
  acting in the interests of national security. The
  courts ruled that national security is, *par excel-
  lence*, a non-justiciable matter, meaning that the

government could do practically anything and escape judicial scrutiny merely by claiming that it was acting in the interests of national security.

Also in the 1980s the courts ruled that the publication by the *Guardian* newspaper of allegations contained in former MI5 officer Peter Wright's book, *Spycatcher*, was unlawful as being in breach of confidence. The law lords were split on this one, ruling by a three-to-two majority in favour of the Thatcher government. One of the dissenting judges spoke with disarming clarity on what he felt about the majority's position. This is what he said:

> Freedom of speech is always the first casualty under a totalitarian regime. Such a regime cannot afford to allow the free circulation of information and ideas among its citizens. Censorship is the indispensable tool to regulate what the public may and what they may not know. The present attempt to insulate the public in this country from information which is freely available elsewhere is a significant step down that very dangerous road. The maintenance of the ban, as more and more copies of . . . *Spycatcher* enter this country and circulate here, will seem more and more ridiculous. [The government's] wafer-thin victory in this litigation has been gained at a price which no government committed to upholding the values of a free society can afford to pay.

Yet even the 'totalitarian regime' of the Thatcher government received support and sustenance from the majority of the judges.

All of these cases were decided before the Human Rights Act 1998 became part of British law. It might be thought that this act would have been an improvement. But this has not been the case. Three cases serve to illustrate the point. The first is *Rehman's case*. Rehman was a Pakistani national who had been given leave to enter and remain in the United Kingdom for a limited period of time. When he applied for indefinite leave to remain his application was refused and the home secretary decided that he should be deported on the ground that he was a danger to national security, as he was alleged to have been involved with rebels in Kashmir. The law lords unanimously refused to quash the home secretary's decision, stating that notwithstanding the fact that 'it cannot be proved . . . that [Rehman] has carried out any individual act which would justify the conclusion that he is a danger', determining that what is in the interests of national security is a matter exclusively for the government of the day, the courts being simply 'not entitled' to disagree with the government's verdict.

In *Shayler's case* the law lords were presented with an opportunity to declare certain provisions of Britain's notorious Official Secrets Act to be incompatible with the right to free speech. The act makes it a criminal offence for a member or former member of the security and intelligence services to disclose any information relating to security or intelligence which came into that person's possession by virtue of his employment in the services. No damage to Britain's national security need actually (or even potentially) be caused by the disclosure and it is no defence that the disclosure was in the public interest (on the ground that, for example, it revealed corruption in the services). The law lords ruled that, notwithstanding the breathtaking scope of this section, it did not breach the right to free speech.

Probably the best known case so far decided under the Human Rights Act is *A v Home Secretary*. This was the decision in December 2004 in which an eight-to-one majority of the law lords held that the government's detention without trial of suspected international terrorists was incompatible with their human rights. Yet even this case reveals the weaknesses inherent in a system which seeks to rely on the judges to secure individual liberty and to hold the government to account. Most of the illegally-held detainees remained in jail for several months following the law lords' ruling. The home secretary then sought to *extend* the coercive reach of the state, as he asked parliament for new powers enabling him to order the house arrest of a *wider* range of people. And even though the government lost some aspects of their argument before the law lords, they actually won the most critical point, the judges holding – despite a severe lack of evidence – that the government was justified in its view (shared by no other state in Europe) that we are in a state of emergency.

It is because of cases such as these that it is dangerous to rely on courts to stop governments. If we want to check government, we will have to do it ourselves, either directly or through elected representatives in our parliaments.

Assessing Parliament

But how effective is political accountability? It is sometimes said that the present position is poor, perhaps even dire. A worst-case diagnosis might run something like this. The British government, re-elected to power in 2001 on little more than 40 per cent of the votes cast in an election in which less than two-thirds of the electorate voted at all, enjoys an enormous majority of seats in the House of Commons – 410 Labour MPs in a House of 659 seats, or 62 per cent. Such a majority hands to the government effective control of the whole of parliament. A Commons that is so dominated by backbench MPs who come from the same political party as forms the government is, it might be thought, a rather unlikely place in which to find effective scrutiny.

While parliament is so weak the government, by contrast, is stronger than ever, or so the worst-case diagnosis would suggest. The government is apparently all-powerful. It may introduce any legislation into either House in any session for any reason. Equally, it may refuse to introduce any legislation, no matter how earnestly desired by the public and no matter how much its enactment may be shown to be for the public good. Such legislation as it does introduce is almost invariably passed, no matter how controversial, illiberal or badly thought through.

The passage of the Anti-terrorism, Crime and Security Act 2001 provides an example. This is the legislation that marked the British government's formal response to 9/11. Despite the fact that it took the government more than two months to prepare the bill, its 129 sections and eight schedules were rushed through parliament in a mere three weeks. The Commons debated the measure for sixteen hours, the Lords for nine days. This, despite the fact that the act is the most draconian piece of legislation passed in peacetime in Britain in over a century.

In 2003 the Blair government took the country into a war with Iraq despite unprecedented opposition internationally, popularly and in parliament. Could any other action so clearly justify the worst-case diagnosis? Internationally, the government failed to persuade many of its key European allies that the war was needed. Nor could the UN security council be cajoled into providing clear authorization for the use of force. At the same time, millions of Britons took to the streets in a series of mass protests against the war and, in parliament, two votes were staged in which unprecedented numbers of Labour MPs voted against the government. These were the biggest backbench rebellions since the passing of the corn laws in the middle of the nineteenth century. Yet despite all of this, the government pressed ahead – military action in Iraq commenced a mere twenty-eight hours after the second Commons vote.

The worst-case diagnosis makes for grim reading, for sure. But does it give a complete view of what has been happening? It seems to us that the position is not actually as bad. Let us take another look at the two events considered above: the passage of the Anti-terrorism legislation in 2001 and the decision to go to war in 2003.

The Anti-terrorism Act is a brutal measure designed, or so the government would have us believe, to counter what is perhaps an even more brutal threat. Notwithstanding the government's repeated warnings about terrorism, however, we should remember that the context in which the 2001 act was passed was that, as the home secretary himself explained in parliament, 'there is no immediate intelligence pointing to a specific threat to the United Kingdom'. Never is it more diffi- cult for parliament to set limits to new executive powers than in times when the government is asserting that national security requires it to possess such powers. Yet despite the fact that it was given only a few hours to debate the bill and despite the fact that the government treated it as an emergency measure, parliament actu- ally did remarkably well in curbing its worst excesses. Several safeguards against abuse of executive powers were added at parliament's insistence. The home secre- tary's powers to detain without trial were watered down. And the act was made subject to a variety of reviews as well as to an eventual sunset clause (so that the powers will lapse after a certain point).

As for the Iraq war, the waging of war is governed
in British constitutional law not by act of parliament
but by the royal prerogative. When the government
commits Britain's armed forces in combat it is exercising Crown power. Parliament's role on such occasions
is limited. But in 2003 there were two votes in the
Commons on the government's proposed use of force
in Iraq. Had the Commons voted against the government's policy, the prime minister would have resigned
from office, or so the media were briefed.

Despite everything, parliament has the means to
check the government of the day. It would have been
easy for parliament to atrophy. The Commons could
easily have been overwhelmed by the unprecedented
weight of Labour's majorities since 1997. The Lords
could equally easily have been silenced by virtue of their
abject lack of democratic authority. But this has not
happened. Parliament generally and the House of
Commons in particular have grown stronger under
Blair. The detailed rules of ministerial responsibility to
parliament were clarified in 1997 in order to prevent
future governments from repeating the constitutional
abuses that occurred under John Major's premiership.
Since 1997 more government bills have been published
in draft, enabling greater parliamentary scrutiny. The
influence of select committees has considerably
increased in recent years. Tony Blair is the first prime
minister in history regularly to give account to a select
committee. When in 2001 the Labour whips tried to
remove certain MPs from the chairs of committees
which had been critical of government policy, the
Commons revolted and the MPs were immediately re-
instated, much to the government's embarrassment. It
was a powerful reminder that these are *parliamentary*
committees and are not the playthings of government.
In October 2003 the Commons voted to pay the senior

and experienced backbench MPs who chair select committees an enhanced salary so that there is now, for the first time, a career structure within the House of Commons that is independent of the pursuit of ministerial office. Finally, there is growing evidence that the Commons is beginning to learn from the experience of the Scottish Parliament and of the National Assembly for Wales, both of which have powerful and sophisticated committee structures designed to secure the political accountability of devolved government.

All of these factors are reasons, if not to be cheerful, then at least to be optimistic. They show that, even under the most demanding of circumstances, parliament has the means to continue to perform its constitutional obligations well. Yet for all these positives, there is so much more that could be done. In the next chapter we sketch out four proposals for reform which are designed to bring the British constitution more fully in line with the republican principles we outlined at the start of this pamphlet.

CHAPTER 5

Republican Reform: Four Proposals

Our four proposals for reform are:

1. We want all of the Crown's prerogative powers to be abolished and, where necessary, replaced with legislation.
2. We want current freedom of information laws to be repealed and replaced with legislation that would secure genuinely open government.
3. We want our parliaments to be reformed so that all are democratically elected and so that all are able to operate freely, without the constraints imposed by party loyalty.
4. We want the Crown and the queen to be removed from the constitution, with the monarch's powers being transferred to the House of Commons.

We will now consider each of these in more detail.

Prerogative Powers

The starting principle for government power should be the same for British government as it already is for local authorities in England and for devolved government in Scotland and Wales: namely, that *the government may exercise* only *those powers which are expressly conferred upon it by statute*.

At the moment the British government has two sorts of powers. It has the powers which are conferred upon it by parliament. But it also has prerogative powers. These are the powers recognized by the law as lying within the authority of the Crown. In former times all prerogative powers were exercised by the monarch him- or herself. But over the centuries, most of these powers have been transferred from monarch to prime minister. A handful of these powers remain with the monarch: only the queen may appoint the prime minister, dismiss the government, dissolve parliament or grant the royal assent that is required for a parliamentary bill to become law.

All other prerogative powers are now exercised by the government. These powers concern an astonishing range of government activity. All of the following fall within the prerogative: the making of treaties, the conduct of diplomacy, the governance of British over-seas territories, the deployment of the armed forces, the appointment and removal of ministers, the appointment of peers, the grant of honours, the organization of the civil service, the issuing of passports and the granting of pardons. In all of these areas the government is free to act – oftentimes in the most coercive manner – without *any* parliamentary approval and, as often as not, without recourse to judicial review. While judicial review of the prerogative is no longer unheard of, most of the government's prerogative powers remain beyond the scrutiny of the courts.

Prerogative powers are not marginal. They concern critical government activities. When Mrs Thatcher banned trade unions from GCHQ, she was using the prerogative. When ministers in John Major's govern-ment issued public interest immunity (PII) certificates in the Matrix Churchill trial on arms-to-Iraq, they were using the prerogative. And when Tony Blair declared war on Iraq, he too was using the prerogative. Yet when exercising such powers ministers have, as a Commons committee recently stated, 'very wide scope to act without parliamentary approval'. And in no area of public law are the courts as reluctant to review government actions and decisions as when they touch upon the prerogative.

The way forward is simple. Parliament should pass a Prerogative (Abolition) Act. The act should contain two sections. Section 1 should provide that 'all prerogative powers shall be abolished' and section 2 should provide (with a nice touch of irony) that 'section 1 shall come into force one year after this act receives the royal assent'. This would give ministers one year in which to introduce legislation that, when passed, would confer on the government such powers as parliament considers it needs in place of its former prerogative powers. There would be a Treaties Act, a Deployment of the Armed Forces Act, a Civil Service Act and so forth, in each of which parliament would lay down the terms according to which the government may exercise its powers. There would also have to be legislation dealing with powers that were formerly exercised by the queen – this issue is considered below.

Open Government

In order for effective scrutiny of government to be possible information about what the government is doing and is proposing to do must be freely available. No system of accountability, whether parliamentary, judicial or of any other kind, can be successful without an informed understanding of what the government is doing. The ideal of republican democracy discussed in Chapter One will remain but that – a mere ideal – without genuinely open government.

While it was in opposition the Labour party appeared to appreciate this. When Labour came to power in 1997 it looked for a while as if it would introduce a sweeping Freedom of Information Act. But within a few months the government suffered a severe change of mind. We do now have a Freedom of Information Act, but as one of Britain's leading freedom of information experts has put it, the act we have amounts to the legislative enshrining of 'a discretionary power to choose what information to disclose' that returns us 'to an all-pervasive culture of secrecy and of seeking to find a reason for not disclosing'. In short, the act is no less than 'a fraud on democratic accountability'. The Freedom of Information (Scotland) Act 2002 is marginally more liberalizing than the British act, but even the Scottish law is half-hearted (at best) about opening up government to public scrutiny.

Given the critical importance of open government and freedom of information, the starting point for reform in this context should be that *all government information is presumed to be open and freely available both to parliament and to the public unless it can be objectively shown and independently verified that its disclosure would cause substantial harm to a specified public good.* The obligation of openness should apply right across government. Exceptions to disclosure should be narrowly drawn and strictly interpreted by an information commissioner appointed by and accountable to parliament.

Parliament and Party

If lack of adequate information is the greatest practical obstacle to securing political accountability, the most significant political impediment lies in the problem of party. Political accountability relies for its success on a separation of interests between ministers and parliamentarians. Party eats away at this separation. Instead of backbench MPs (or MSPs) being constitutionally loyal to the public good, they become loyal to their parties. If their political party is in power, party loyalty dictates that they support the government regardless of the greater public good. Conversely, if their party is in opposition, MPs obstruct government policy for the sake of party political point-scoring, even where the government is acting for the public good.

We saw in the previous chapter that since 2001 the House of Commons has witnessed a series of back-bench rebellions against the government. More gener-ally the growing prominence of the all-party Commons select committees has established a healthy working pattern of cross-party backbench scrutiny of govern-ment policy. In this sense there are already in the House of Commons a number of ways in which parliamen-tarians find themselves not being governed only, or even mainly, by party loyalty. Welcome though this is, however, as things stand there is no way of *guaranteeing* that MPs will not allow loyalty to party to obstruct loyalty to parliament's constitutional function. What is needed, therefore, is just such a guarantee – some method of preventing party from replacing the public good as the interest for which MPs work.

What is required is the removal of blind party loyalty from the working of our parliaments. Whips should be prohib-ited. There should be no whipped votes. There should be no whips' offices through which parliamentary office-holding (such as the chairing of select committees) can be fixed. There should be no institutional means – save for seeking to justify the merits of their policies in open parliamentary debate – by which the government is able to secure parliamentary support. At first sight this may appear an implausible suggestion. We readily admit – indeed we hope – that if implemented it would bring about radical changes in the ways in which our parlia-ments work, particularly on the floor of the House of

Commons. But as the last twenty years' experience of select committees shows, it is not a suggestion that flies in the face of everything the British parliament currently stands for.

The Crown

The final item on our reform agenda returns to the monarchy. There are all sorts of reasons, some stronger than others, as to why the British monarchy should be abolished. The degrading rituals of pomp and circumstance that surround the queen and her entourage. The way in which generations of the royal family have sought ways of limiting their contributions to the exchequer. The unhelpful political interventions of various princes on matters as wide-ranging as architecture, town planning, agriculture and blood sports. All of these and more have contributed in recent years to a growing sense of popular restlessness that the royals have outlived their usefulness.

But even if the first family were composed of the brightest and most virtuous of Britons, there would still be two compelling reasons for abolishing the Crown. The first is that the existence of the Crown is incompatible with our political freedom. *Being subjects of the Crown rather than citizens of a republic reduces us to the status of slaves.* The second reason is that the Crown simply gets in the way of the constitutional project of trying to find ways of holding the government to account. Neither our parliaments nor the courts are in a position to review or scrutinize any power exercised by the queen herself. And both political and legal institutions have struggled, not particularly successfully, to bring the ministerial exercise of prerogative power within the scope of their overview. The abolition of the Crown would bring about the strengthening of

both parliamentary and judicial review of government
action.

One question that naturally follows from advocating
that the Crown be abolished is what it should be
replaced with. Our answer is that there is no need to
create any new office as a replacement. The constitutional powers of the queen should simply be transferred
to the House of Commons. Either parliament could
legislate to place the queen's powers on a statutory basis,
to be exercised on parliament's behalf by the speaker
of the House of Commons – that is, by the member
of the House freely elected by the House as a whole to
represent its interests. Or parliament could legislate so
as to remove the need for the powers. Instead of it being
in the queen's discretion when to dissolve parliament
and call a general election, we could move to fixed-term
sessions, as we already have for local and devolved
authorities. Similarly, instead of it being in the queen's
discretion whom should be appointed as prime minister, parliament could pass an act providing that the MP
able to command majority support in the Commons
shall assume the office of prime minister for as long as
such support remains. Statutes could become law upon
their passage through parliament with no need for any
third-party assent.

Constitutionally we do not need the queen. Nor do
we need any presidential head of state to replace her.
All the monarch's constitutional powers could – and
should – be vested in parliament. In a republican constitution what we *do* need is a strong parliament, able fully
and properly to represent the sovereign authority of the
people. To this end, *all* the government's powers should
be derived from parliament and the government should
be responsible to parliament for the exercise of *all* of
its powers, irrespective of subject-matter.

CONCLUSION

What Should We All Do Now?

Even without the reforms of the previous chapter, there is no excuse for inaction. As Edmund Burke is often said to have remarked, 'all that has to happen for evil to triumph is for good men to do nothing'. We believe that we are a sovereign people. If we are unhappy with our present system of government in Britain, all that stops us from acting to change it is our own laziness or lack of imagination.

In the immediate future we should take part as widely as possible in the coming general election. At the minimum, this means we should vote. We should talk, publicly and privately, about what we want. We should campaign. We should harangue the powerful and speak up for what we believe. When young William Pitt was out of office and wanted parliament reformed he advised like-minded folk to form clubs and join associations to petition parliament and lobby for change.

So vote! Speak! Make sure that your representatives in parliament represent what you want. If you want accountable government, vote for an MP who will insist our government accounts for itself: not for one who will merely obey a party's managers. It is *your sovereign right* to have a government that answers to *you*. And it is your sovereign right to have a parliament that works tirelessly to make sure this happens.

We are a sovereign people. So let's act like one.

Select Bibliography

Cases:

A v. Home Secretary [2004] U.K.H.L. 56
Attorney-General v. Guardian Newspapers [1987] 3 All E.R. 316
Home Secretary v. Rehman [2003] 1 A.C. 153
R v. Shayler [2003] 1 A.C. 247

Books and Articles:

Austin, Rodney, 'The Freedom of Information Act 2000', in J. Jowell and D. Oliver (eds), *The Changing Constitution* (Oxford UP, 2004, 5th ed)

Candappa, Rohan, *The Curious Incident of the WMD in Iraq* (Profile Books, 2004)

Harrington, James, *The Commonwealth of Oceana* [1656] (ed. J.G.A. Pocock, Cambridge UP, 1992)

Harris, John, *So Now Who Do We Vote For?* (Faber and Faber, 2005)

Locke, John, *Two Treatises of Government* [1690] (ed. P. Laslett, Cambridge UP, 1960)

Machiavelli, Niccolo, *The Discourses* [1517] (ed. B. Crick and trans. L.J. Walker, Penguin, 1998)

Mathieson, William Law, *Scotland and the Union* (J. Maclehose, 1905)

Milton, John, *Areopagitica and other Political Writings* (ed. J. Alvis, Liberty Fund, 1999)

Paine, Thomas, *The Rights of Man* (J. S. Jordan, 1791)

Pettit, Philip, *Republicanism: A Theory of Freedom and Government* (Oxford UP, 1997)

Prebble, John, *The Lion in the North* (Secker and Warburg, 1971)

Scruton, Roger, *England: an Elegy* (Chatto & Windus, 2000)

Sidney, Algernon, *Discourses Concerning Government* [1683] (ed. T. West, Liberty Fund, 1996)

Skinner, Quentin, *Liberty before Liberalism* (Cambridge UP, 1997)

Spitz, Jean-Fabien, 'The Twilight of the Republic', in D. Weinstock and C. Nadeau (eds), *Republicanism: History, Theory and Practice* (Frank Cass, 2004)

Tomkins, Adam, *Our Republican Constitution* (Hart Publishing, 2005)

—, *Public Law* (Oxford UP, 2003)

—, *The Constitution after Scott* (Oxford UP, 1998)

Weiler, J.H.H., *The Constitution of Europe* (Cambridge UP, 1999)

Wright, Peter, *Spycatcher* (Viking, 1987)